Dance in a Buffalo Skull

Dance in a Buffalo Skull

—

by Zitkala-Ša

—

Illustrated by S. D. Nelson

—

A Prairie Tale

SOUTH DAKOTA STATE HISTORICAL SOCIETY PRESS
PIERRE

A PRAIRIE TALE FROM THE
SOUTH DAKOTA STATE HISTORICAL SOCIETY PRESS

Editor: Nancy Tystad Koupal, Introduction: Martyn Beeny
Graphic Design: Mark Conahan, Production Manager: Patti Edman

The text of "Dance in a Buffalo Skull" was originally published in
Old Indian Legends in 1901.

Dance in a Buffalo Skull is Volume 2 in the Prairie Tale series.

This publication is funded, in part, by
the Great Plains Education Foundation, Inc., Aberdeen, S.Dak.
The South Dakota Arts Council provided support for the artwork with funds
from the State of South Dakota, through the Department of Tourism and
State Development, and the National Endowment for the Arts.

Library of Congress Cataloging-in-Publication data
Zitkala-Ša, 1876-1938.
Dance in a buffalo skull / by Zitkala-Ša; illustrated by S. D. Nelson.
p. cm. – (Prairie tales from the South Dakota State Historical
Society Press; v. 2)
Includes bibliographical references.
ISBN 978-0-9777955-2-9
1. Yankton Indians—Folklore. 2. Tales—South Dakota.
I. Nelson, S.D., ill. II. Title.

E99.Y25Z58 2007
398.209783–dc22
2007007099
Printed in Canada
11 10 09 08 07 1 2 3 4 5

Introduction

ZITKALA-ŠA WAS BORN in 1876 on the Yankton Sioux Indian Reservation in South Dakota. As a little girl, she listened to the Elders of her tribe tell stories around the campfire. One of her favorite stories was about a wildcat, some mice, and an old buffalo skull. She loved the story and wrote it down in English for others to enjoy as she did.

Dance in a Buffalo Skull is an old, old tale. Zitkala-Ša tried to write it down as she had heard it around the campfire. The animals and the places are the same. The mice live on a grassy prairie in an area known as the Great Plains. The same scary eyes flash, and the wolves howl just as Zitkala-Ša remembered them.

Animals were always important in American Indian stories. The Elders used them to teach lessons to children who lived on the open prairie. In this story, the mice are enjoying the dance, but they are enjoying it too much. No one is keeping watch. Children who live in a wild country must always be alert for danger. They must have an escape plan.

The Great Plains of the United States have changed since the Elders first told this tale. They have changed even more since Zitkala-Ša wrote the story down over one hundred years ago. Wolves no longer howl in the dark of night, and wildcats rarely slink along the riverbeds. Most of the buffalo have gone, too. It is hard to find a dried buffalo skull now. The country is not so wild, but some things do not change. Mice still need to be wary of cats and dogs.

The Sioux Indians, also known as the Dakota, Lakota, or Nakota Indians, told each other this story over and over. This way of teaching and sharing information is called oral history. The lessons always come through to the listeners. Those lessons are still important today. We all need to pay attention to the world around us and not get too caught up in what we are doing.

IT WAS NIGHT upon the prairie. Overhead the stars were twinkling bright their red and yellow lights.

The moon was young. A silvery thread among the
stars, it soon drifted low beneath the horizon.

Upon the ground the land was pitchy black. There are
night people on the plain who love the dark. Amid
the black level land they meet to frolic under the stars.

Then when their sharp ears hear any strange footfalls
nigh they scamper away into the deep shadows
of night. There they are safely hid from all dangers,
they think.

Thus it was that one very black night, afar off from the edge of the level land, out of the wooded river bottom glided forth two balls of fire.

They came farther and farther into the level land.
They grew larger and brighter. The dark hid the body
of the creature with those fiery eyes.

They came on and on, just over the tops of the prairie grass. It might have been a wildcat prowling low on soft, stealthy feet. Slowly but surely the terrible eyes drew nearer and nearer to the heart of the level land.

There in a huge old buffalo skull was a gay feast and dance! Tiny little field mice were singing and dancing in a circle to the boom-boom of a wee, wee drum.

They were laughing and talking among themselves
while their chosen singers sang loud a merry tune.

They built a small open fire within the center of their queer dance house. The light streamed out of the buffalo skull through all the curious sockets and holes.

A light on the plain in the middle of the night was an unusual thing. But so merry were the mice they did not hear the "kins, kins" of sleepy birds, disturbed by the unaccustomed fire.

A pack of wolves, fearing to come nigh this night fire, stood together a little distance away, and, turning their pointed noses to the stars, howled and yelped most dismally. Even the cry of the wolves was unheeded by the mice within the lighted buffalo skull.

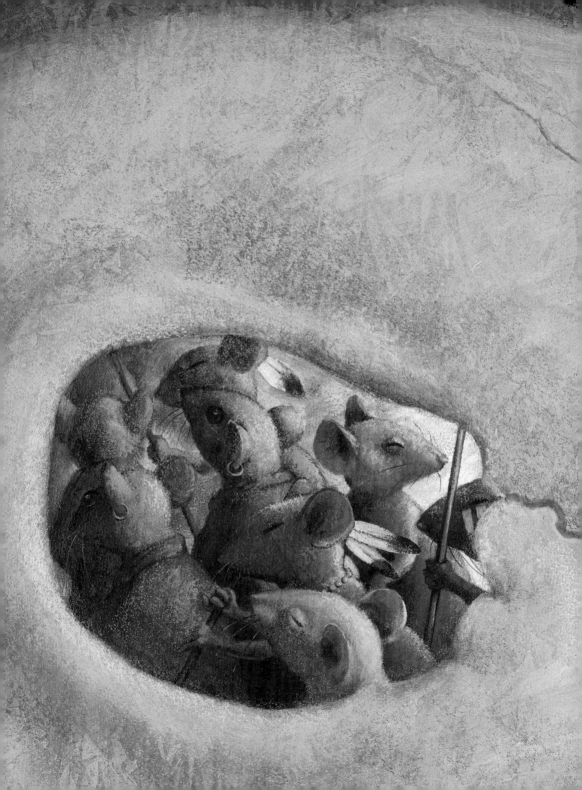

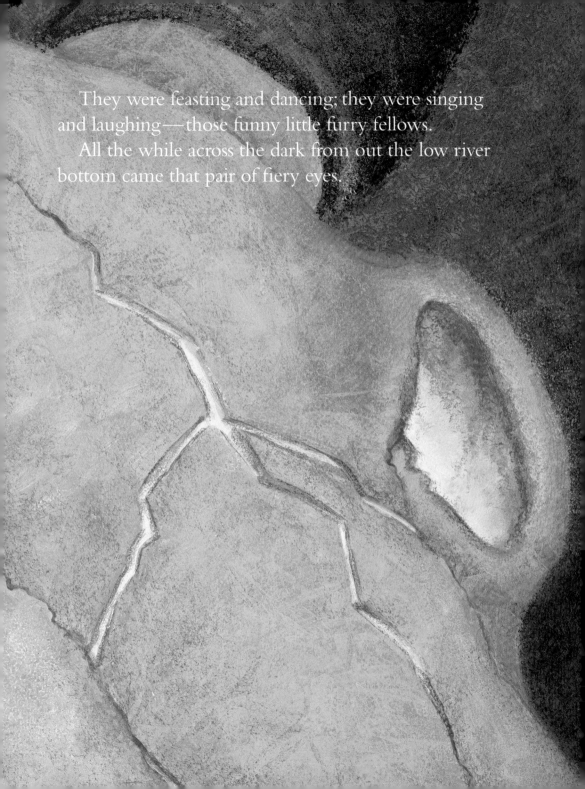

They were feasting and dancing; they were singing
and laughing—those funny little furry fellows.

All the while across the dark from out the low river
bottom came that pair of fiery eyes.

Now closer and more swift, now fiercer and
glaring, the eyes moved toward the buffalo skull.
All unconscious of those fearful eyes, the happy
mice nibbled at dried roots and venison.

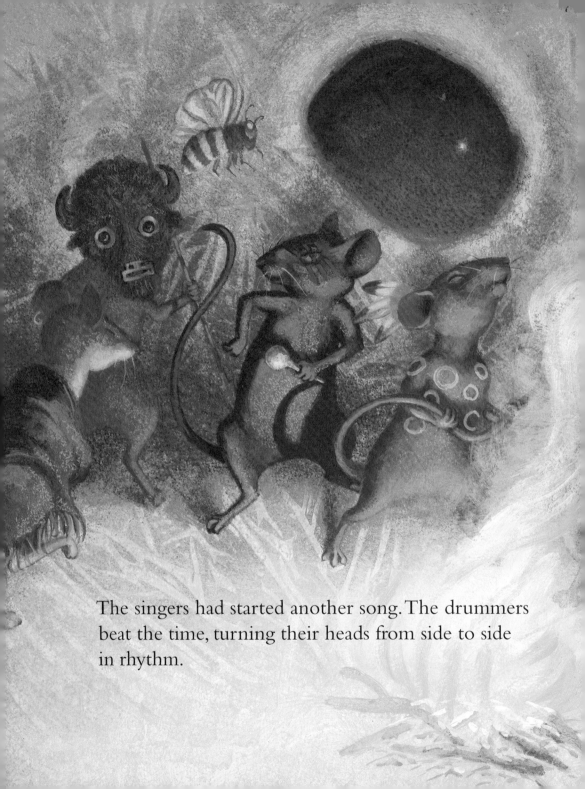

The singers had started another song. The drummers
beat the time, turning their heads from side to side
in rhythm.

In a ring around the fire hopped the mice, each bouncing hard on his two hind feet. Some carried their tails over their arms, while others trailed them proudly along.

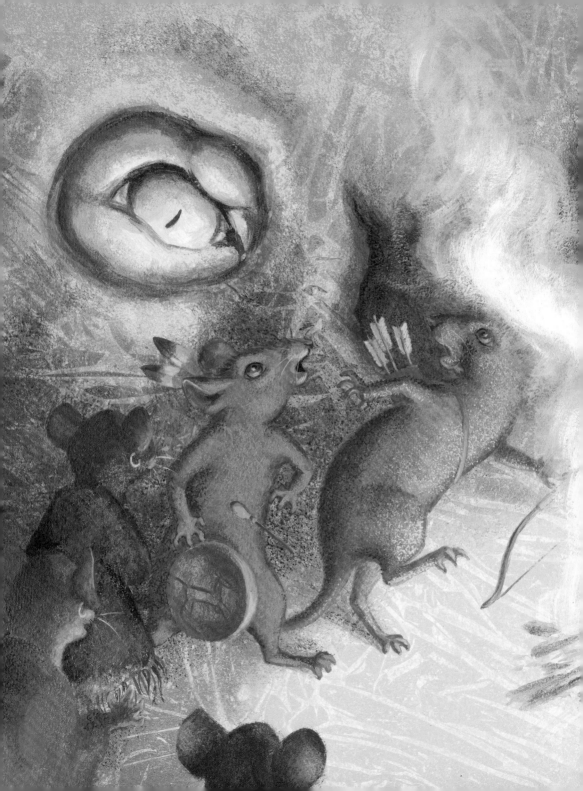

Ah, very near are those round yellow eyes! Very low
to the ground they seem to creep—creep toward
the buffalo skull. All of a sudden they slide into the
eye-sockets of the old skull.

"Spirit of the buffalo!" squeaked a frightened
mouse as he jumped out from a hole in the back part
of the skull.

"A cat! a cat!" cried other mice as they scrambled
out of holes both large and snug.

Noiseless they ran away into the dark.

The End

Word list

dismally—with sadness
disturbed—scared; startled
frolic—dance and play; have fun
gay—happy
horizon—where the land and
the sky meet
nigh—close by; near
pitchy—as dark as tar
prowling—moving around
in search of something
queer—strange
stealthy—quiet
unaccustomed—not usual
unconscious—not aware of
unheeded—not paid
attention to
venison—deer meat

Bibliography

Fisher, Dexter. "Zitkala-Ša: The Evolution of a Writer." *American Indian Quarterly* 5 (Aug. 1979): 229-38.

Kilcup, Karen L., ed. *Native American Women's Writing, c. 1800-1924: An Anthology*. Oxford: Blackwell Publishers, 2000.

Zitkala-Ša. *American Indian Stories*. Washington: Hayworth Publishing House, 1921.

Zitkala-Ša. *Dreams and Thunder: Stories, Poems, and The Sun Dance Opera*. Ed. P. Jane Hafen. Lincoln: University of Nebraska Press, 2001.

Zitkala-Ša. *Old Indian Legends*. Boston: Ginn & Co., 1901.